ideals®
FRIENDSHIP
2005

Dedicated to a celebration of the American ideals of faith in God, loyalty to country, and love of family.

Features

Departments

Cover: A generous bouquet of summer flowers fills a day with color. Photograph by Nancy Matthews.

Inside front cover: Two lovely young friends enjoy a walk together in this painting entitled AT THE STILE, by Henry John Yeend King (1855-1924). Image from Fine Art Photographic Library Ltd., London/Fine Art of Oakham.

IDEALS—Vol. 62, No. 4 July 2005 IDEALS (ISSN 0019-137X, USPS 256-240) is published six times a year: January, March, May, July, September, and November by Ideals Publications, a division of Guideposts, 39 Seminary Hill Road, Carmel, NY 10512. Copyright © 2005 by Ideals Publications, a division of Guideposts. All rights reserved. The cover and entire contents of IDEALS are fully protected by copyright and must not be reproduced in any manner whatsoever. Title IDEALS registered U.S. Patent Office. Printed and bound in USA. Printed on Weyerhaeuser Husky. The paper used in this publication meets the minimum requirements of American National Standard for Information Sciences—Permanence of Paper for Printed Library Materials, ANSI Z39.48-1984. Periodicals postage paid at Carmel, New York, and additional mailing offices. Canadian mailed under Publications Mail Agreement Number 40010140. POSTMASTER: Send address changes to IDEALS, 39 Seminary Hill Road, Carmel, NY 10512. CANADA POST: Send address changes to Guideposts PO Box 1051, Fort Erie ON L2A 6C7. For subscription or customer service questions, contact Ideals Publications, a division of Guideposts, 39 Seminary Hill Road, Carmel, NY 10512. Fax 845-228-2115. Reader Preference Service: We occasionally make our mailing lists available to other companies whose products or services might interest you. If you prefer not to be included, please write to Ideals Customer Service.

ISBN 0-8249-1303-5 GST 893989236

For subscription information and submission guidelines, visit www.idealsbooks.com

A Priceless Gift
Erla Huber Martin

Friendship is a priceless gift,
A cherished bond of caring,
That grows richer day by day
By smiling, loving, sharing.
Friends have the special closeness
That two human hearts may share.
Their trust and admiration
Are mixed with love and prayer.
True friends can make you happy,
Support you through your sorrow;

Their smiles uplift your spirits,
Bringing hope of bright tomorrows.
There's giving and there's taking,
There's talking and listening too.
For this brings understanding
That makes a bond grow strong.
A sincere and loyal friend
Lets you dare to be yourself
And is a special gift
That exceeds all earthly wealth.

Moments to Cherish
June Masters Bacher

Sweet yesterday's left us;
That is quite clear.
Tomorrow is coming.
This day is here,
So come walk with me
For part of the way.
God willing, together
We'll share today.
What matter beginnings?
What matter ends?
What's precious are moments
Spent with our friends.

*Lilies, sweet William, lady's mantle, feverfew, and allium
create a beautiful rainbow of colors in a garden.
Photograph by Mary Liz Austin/Donnelly Austin Photography.*

A Special Wish
Virginia Richardson

May you always walk where flowers bloom
With a sky of blue above you;
May you always have a heart that sings
And faithful friends to love you;
May you have so many joys to reap,
There'll be no time for pining;
And if a cloud should happen by,
May it have a silver lining.

Three Joys
Carice Williams

I count this day a special day
Because I made a friend,
A friend to share my future days
And happiness extend.
I count this day a special day
Because, as I walked by,
There was a garden filled with blooms
Whose beauty caught my eye.

I count this day a special day
That filled my heart with cheer
Because a cardinal in a tree
Brought music to my ear.
A friend, a flower, a cheerful song
That chanced to come my way
Have brought me joy and helped create
The best of all my days.

Oh, the comfort—the inexpressible comfort of feeling safe with a person—having neither to weigh thoughts nor measure words, but pouring them all right out, just as they are, chaff and grain together, certain that a faithful hand will take and sift them, keep what is worth keeping, and with the breath of kindness blow the rest away. —Dinah Maria Mulock Craik

Vivid yellow and pink blossoms brighten this garden wall.
Photograph by Nancy Matthews.

BE COURTEOUS TO ALL, BUT INTIMATE WITH FEW;
AND LET THOSE FEW BE WELL TRIED BEFORE YOU
GIVE THEM YOUR CONFIDENCE. TRUE FRIENDSHIP
IS A PLANT OF SLOW GROWTH AND MUST UNDERGO
AND WITHSTAND THE SHOCKS OF ADVERSITY
BEFORE IT IS ENTITLED TO THE APPELLATION.
—GEORGE WASHINGTON

The Tree

Minnie Klemme

I think of friendship as a tree
That grows in sun or shade:
From seedling to sapling to gnarled old age,
Growth rings added, season to season.
Rooted deep in the heart's bedrock,
This tree holds fast in storm or stress:
It bends with the wind; it does not break.
Friendship seen as a flower is lovely;
But I like to see it as a tree
That greens for all eternity.

A Sheltering Tree

Samuel Taylor Coleridge

Flowers are lovely; love is flower-like;
Friendship is a sheltering tree;
Oh, the joys that came down shower-like,
Of friendship, love, and liberty
Ere I was old!

*A scarlet horse chestnut tree shades a park bench at the Hiram M. Chittenden Locks
in Seattle, Washington. Photograph by Terry Donnelly/Donnelly Austin Photography.*

DEVOTIONS FROM THE HEART

Pamela Kennedy

Perfume and incense bring joy to the heart, and the pleasantness of one's friend springs from his earnest counsel. —*Proverbs 27:9* (NIV)

FRAGRANT FRIENDSHIP

Come on, let's go walking early tomorrow morning." My friend called to encourage me to get up and exercise because I had been complaining about the way my clothes fit.

"You know, when our son was in the same situation, this is what worked for us." A friend offered some timely advice after I shared a concern about our adult offspring.

"There is no sense in beating yourself up about it. It is over and done. Pick up the pieces and move on." A colleague offered some good advice when one of my assignments had not worked out quite the way I had hoped.

"Have you ever considered that he did not mean it that way? Perhaps he is just concerned about you and is trying to help." A mentor offered an alternative perspective when I took offense at the words of a relative.

There are so many times when I have needed the wise words of a friend to encourage me, to get my thoughts back on track, or to help me contemplate my options when I am making a decision. I know I can operate on my own; but I also know that sometimes I get lost in the muddle of my own thoughts, and a good friend helps to bring perspective and sharpen my focus.

Good friends do that for us. They love us enough to get involved, to offer advice, and to make helpful observations. Giving counsel is a risky business. What if you say the wrong thing? What if your friend gets upset? What if she does not want to hear what you have to offer? Those are all real possibilities, yet I think a true friend is willing to take those risks.

The proverb of wise king Solomon pairs the

Dear Lord, help me to be a fragrant friend. May the words I share bring joy to my friend's heart. And may I have the humility to listen when she shares earnest counsel with me. Amen.

statement about the earnest counsel of a friend with an observation about perfume and incense. What an unusual combination . . . or is it? Perfume and incense arouse our senses, focus our thoughts, and linger long after the source is gone. Is not good counsel just like that? Initially when we hear words of counsel, we might become a bit defensive or uneasy. We may even feel relieved or concerned. But then we really think about the

This lovely cottage kitchen, with its hand-painted decorative touches, welcomes friends to the table. Photograph by Jessie Walker.

advice our friends have given us. We examine their words from different angles and explore new possibilities for our current situation. Then, days or hours later, we integrate those suggestions into our own circumstances. We accept what we feel may help, and we modify or even discard other parts; yet the results are often the same as those Solomon describes: joy is produced in our hearts. We find joy in knowing that someone cares about us enough to help us improve, to lift a concern, or to change our outlook.

So many people in our world live isolated, independent lives and are unwilling to risk establishing deep, trusting friendships. But it is through friendship that God touches our hearts with His care and concern. Through the voices of good friends, He reassures us that we are valued and loved. In a society that values rugged individualism, dependence upon one another is sometimes discounted as a weakness. But if we want the sweet perfume of friendship to scent our relationships, we need to be willing both to receive and share earnest counsel as friends. The Scriptures remind us that we please God when we love one another in words and in deeds. Are you willing to both accept and offer fragrant friendship?

Pamela Kennedy is a freelance writer of short stories, articles, essays, and children's books. Wife of a retired naval officer and mother of three children, she has made her home on both U.S. coasts and currently resides in Honolulu, Hawaii.

There is no friend like an old friend
who has shared our morning days,

Friends

Margaret Rorke

Our early friendships never fade,
    Nor do they split from wear.
The threads from which these bonds are made
    Are memories we share.

Those memories contain a strength
    Akin to strength of youth
That, as the years increase in length,
    Intensifies this truth.

Much sharper to the aging eye
    Are trials a long time spent.
Much clearer are the days gone by,
    With laughter lightly lent,

Than what is going on right now
    When problems posed are real
And time's too hurried to allow
    The furrowed brow to feel.

We may not meet or clasp the hand
    Or even ply the pen,
But still we're sure folks understand
    Who knew us way back when

Because there pulls a tighter tie
    To old friends than to new;
And they'll agree and tell you why:
    They share those memories too.

no greeting like his welcome,
no homage like his praise.
—Oliver Wendell Holmes Jr.

Lavender windflowers provide delicate color in the garden.
Photograph by LeFever/Grushow/Grant Heilman Photography.

FOR THE CHILDREN

Come Play

Eileen Spinelli

Come play with me.
Let's have a race
    around the block.
Let's go someplace—
    like your back yard.
Let's make a tent—
    this blanket would be
    excellent.
Do you like fishing
    in the creek?
Or riding bikes?
Or hide-and-seek?
I've got some paper,
    pencils too.
I think it's fun
    to draw. Do you?
And I'd be glad
    to share my box
    of dinosaurs
    and building blocks.
Or we could watch
    a video,
Or learn to do
    a magic show,
Or make a game
    of "let's pretend."
Come play with me.
Come be my friend.

Sharing new shoes with a friend is an important event in this
painting by Donald Zolan entitled New Shoes. *Copyright ©*
Pemberton & Oakes Ltd. Used with permission.

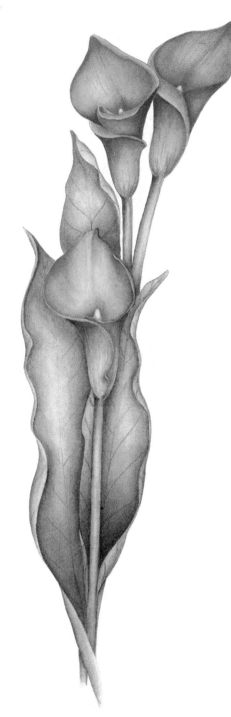

Ones Held Dear

Blanche Garretson

There is comfort in old friendships
That I find hard to beat;
A lovely, warm companionship
Exists when old friends meet:
No awkward introductions,
No need to break the ice,
And no disguising feelings
In an effort to be nice.
With a bond of long-shared memories,
Of laughter, maybe tears,
There is a depth of understanding
Developed over many years.
A sort of "old shoe" comfort comes
From feelings that you share;
Each friend's just glad in knowing
That the other one is near,
An interlude of pleasure to
Remember when apart.
Old friends may leave your presence,
But they never leave your heart.

A variegated canna lily and a birdhouse decorate this garden in Provincetown, Massachusetts. Photograph by Mary Liz Austin/Donnelly Austin Photography.

Early Friendship

Stephen E. Spring Rice

The half-seen memories of childish days
    When pains and pleasures lightly came and went;
    The sympathies of boyhood rashly spent
In fearful wanderings through forbidden ways;
The vague, but manly, wish to tread the maze
    Of life to noble ends; whereon intent,
    Asking to know for what man here is sent,
The bravest heart must often pause, and gaze—
The firm resolve to seek the chosen end
    Of manhood's judgment, cautious and mature:
Each of these viewless bonds binds friend to friend
    With strength no selfish purpose can secure;
My happy lot is this, that all attend
    That friendship which first came,
        and which shall last endure.

*This lovely field of cosmos, poppies, and other wildflowers
would tickle the toes of any barefooted child.
Photograph by William H. Johnson.*

17

SLICE OF LIFE

Anne Campbell

TO AN OLD FRIEND

Out of the sunny past you came,
Calling me by my childhood name,
Bringing me meadows rich with wheat,
The sheltered lane and the cool retreat.
Out of the land of used to be,
You smiled and gave your hand to me.
Under your spell, I saw once more
The garden gate and the farmhouse door.

Once in a distant glowing time,
Shoulder to shoulder we used to climb.
Green was the hill and the path curved high
To the turquoise arch of the friendly sky.
Gone is the farmhouse and the grove;
Gone are the landmarks we used to love;
Gone is our footprint on the hill;
Only our friendship lingers still!

*A young lady has a special friend in Robert
Duncan's painting entitled BEST FRIENDS.
Image provided by Robert Duncan Studios.*

BACKYARD CALENDAR

Joan Donaldson

As I pull open the wooden gate to my garden, I notice a large spider web sparkling in the morning sunshine. Often the humid days of August give way to cool evenings thick with dew, a reminder that the earth is turning. These last weeks of summer are a time to gather and share the abundant harvest that surrounds me.

From my garden shed, I haul our half-bushel baskets and deposit them at the ends of various rows. The seedling tomatoes I patted into the earth in May rise five feet from their staked positions. Red, pink, and orange globes cascade in clusters on bent branches. Cherry tomatoes shine like Christmas ornaments. Slowly, I pluck the ripe fruit, some squatty and oval, others plum-shaped, and heap them in my baskets. Most of these tomatoes will be transformed into salsa or soup, and already many rosy pints and quarts line the shelves of my pantry. Some of the fruit will be sent home with friends who drop by.

This corner of the garden is smothered in squash vines, and maroon and yellow striped sunflower blossoms ramble about. Goldfinches rest upon the spent flowers, pulling out seeds, gleaning from what I nurtured. They help me control the number of seeds that will fall and sprout next year as volunteers.

The sunflowers are not the only flowers that add color. Everywhere I look, the garden is lush. Bright zinnias and cosmos spill a rainbow of color, and white foamy blossoms rise from the feathery coriander plants. The hum of bees drifts from the purple spires of the anise hyssop. The urge to plant "just a little more" has resulted in beds covered with both blossoms and produce.

One of the joys of gardening is observing how the offerings of seeds and cuttings from friends and fellow gardeners shape the nature of this year's garden. Heirloom bean seeds collected by a friend in Minnesota and hyssop seeds from a friend in Vermont have fulfilled their promise. The rose cuttings that arrived

Although we live hundreds of miles apart, our love for one another and gardening binds us together.

from another gardener in South Carolina now twine through the slatted board fence. I like to muse on how my gifts of cuttings or seed envelopes have enhanced my friends' gardens. Although we live hundreds of miles apart, our love for one another and gardening binds us together.

When I finish picking the tomatoes, I set the full baskets in the shade of the rose arbor. Then I wade into a sea of vines that are dotted with yellow star-shaped flowers. Surveying the

A rustic cedar chair invites relaxation in this beautiful private garden in Missouri. Photograph by Gay Bumgarner.

tangle of cantaloupe melons, I inhale their spicy fragrance. The vines crawl across the paths and through the fence. For weeks I have lifted leaves, eyed the swelling melons, and tried to estimate when they would ripen. Now the time has arrived for the first fruits to be chilled and savored. As I fill several baskets, I mentally list the friends who do not have gardens and would welcome a cantaloupe for dessert.

The voices of the goldfinches warble from the sunflowers as I begin to tote baskets of produce to the house. The late summer sun has moved high in the sky and burned the dew from the leaves and cobwebs.

While listening to the drone of the crickets, I preserve memories of the bees in the hyssop and the taste of the heirloom beans that came from plants grown from my friends' generous gifts of seeds. I hope that from their own gardens these loved ones will harvest the same joy.

Joan Donaldson is the author of a picture book and a young adult novel, as well as essays that have appeared in national publications. She and her husband raised their sons on Pleasant Hill Farm in Michigan, where they continue to practice rural skills.

The Gift
Pauline Havard

She brought me yellow roses, a floral gift
That never fails to give the heart a lift,
Essence of summer with its warm, gold light,
Their fragrance sweet and petals
    a breathtaking sight.
I think, as I put the roses into a bowl,
How much an armful of beauty warms the soul,
This gift of loveliness from friend to friend.
Rich is the giver with rose blooms to spend,
And rich is the recipient who sets each bloom
In a treasured place to light her room.

*Gold is the gift of vanity and common
pride, but flowers are the gift of love
and friendship.* —Franz Grillparzer

To a Friend
Roy Z. Kemp

Of all the gifts that life may bring,
    Your friendship's treasured most of all.
It is a lovely, gracious thing
    And steadies me when I would fall.

It comforts me when I know tears
    And keeps my feet from paths of wrong;
It strengthens me when there are fears
    And keeps my spirit stout and strong.

Your friendship is a valued part
    That helps my faith each passing day.
It is a treasure in my heart;
    I'm glad we walk in friendship's way.

*Exquisite yellow roses are the perfect gift
for a friend. Photograph by Nancy Matthews.*

FAMILY RECIPES

The gift of food is always a special way to show appreciation to friends. As your friends gather around your table, share these recipes from the IDEALS' family of readers. We would love to try your favorite recipe too. Send a typed copy to Ideals Publications, 535 Metroplex Drive, Suite 250, Nashville, Tennessee 37211. Payment will be provided for each recipe published.

CHEESE DROPS

Nancy C. Cox, Ridgeway, Virginia

8 tablespoons butter, softened
1 cup grated sharp Cheddar cheese
1 cup flour
⅛ teaspoon cayenne pepper
1 cup crisp rice cereal

Preheat oven to 350°F. In a large bowl, stir butter and cheese until smooth and creamy. In small bowl, stir together flour and cayenne until well combined. Add dry mixture to creamed mixture; stir until dry ingredients are well moistened. Stir in crisp rice cereal; mix until thoroughly combined. Drop from a rounded teaspoon onto an ungreased cookie sheet. Bake 15 to 20 minutes. Makes 2 dozen.

FRIED SUMMER SQUASH

Sherry Timberman, Sanford, Maine

1 unpeeled crookneck or zucchini squash
½ cup flour
½ cup grated Cheddar cheese
½ teaspoon salt
⅛ teaspoon pepper
2 tablespoons butter
1 egg, beaten

Cut squash into ½-inch thick slices. In a medium bowl, combine flour, cheese, salt, and pepper; mix well. Melt butter in a medium-hot skillet. Dip squash into egg, then into flour mixture. Brown squash lightly on both sides. Makes 4 servings.

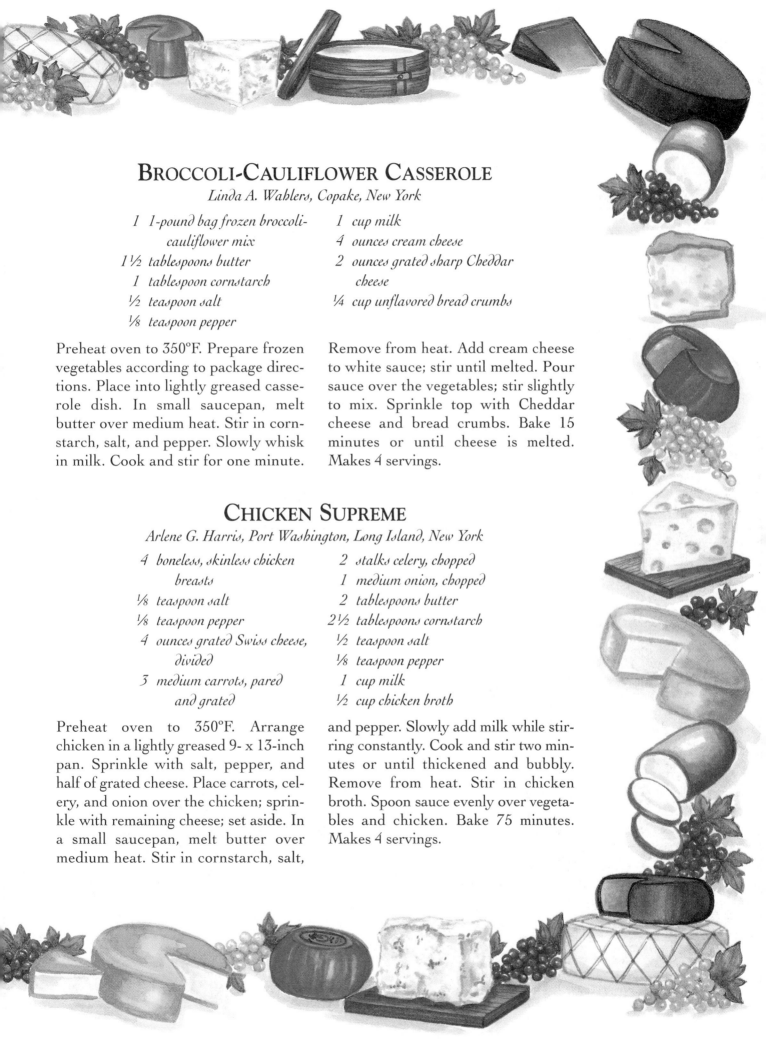

BROCCOLI-CAULIFLOWER CASSEROLE

Linda A. Wahlers, Copake, New York

1   1-pound bag frozen broccoli-
      cauliflower mix
1½ tablespoons butter
1   tablespoon cornstarch
½   teaspoon salt
⅛   teaspoon pepper

1   cup milk
4   ounces cream cheese
2   ounces grated sharp Cheddar
      cheese
¼   cup unflavored bread crumbs

Preheat oven to 350°F. Prepare frozen vegetables according to package directions. Place into lightly greased casserole dish. In small saucepan, melt butter over medium heat. Stir in cornstarch, salt, and pepper. Slowly whisk in milk. Cook and stir for one minute.

Remove from heat. Add cream cheese to white sauce; stir until melted. Pour sauce over the vegetables; stir slightly to mix. Sprinkle top with Cheddar cheese and bread crumbs. Bake 15 minutes or until cheese is melted. Makes 4 servings.

CHICKEN SUPREME

Arlene G. Harris, Port Washington, Long Island, New York

4   boneless, skinless chicken
      breasts
⅛   teaspoon salt
⅛   teaspoon pepper
4   ounces grated Swiss cheese,
      divided
3   medium carrots, pared
      and grated

2   stalks celery, chopped
1   medium onion, chopped
2   tablespoons butter
2½ tablespoons cornstarch
½   teaspoon salt
⅛   teaspoon pepper
1   cup milk
½   cup chicken broth

Preheat oven to 350°F. Arrange chicken in a lightly greased 9- x 13-inch pan. Sprinkle with salt, pepper, and half of grated cheese. Place carrots, celery, and onion over the chicken; sprinkle with remaining cheese; set aside. In a small saucepan, melt butter over medium heat. Stir in cornstarch, salt,

and pepper. Slowly add milk while stirring constantly. Cook and stir two minutes or until thickened and bubbly. Remove from heat. Stir in chicken broth. Spoon sauce evenly over vegetables and chicken. Bake 75 minutes. Makes 4 servings.

THE ENDEARING ELEGANCE OF

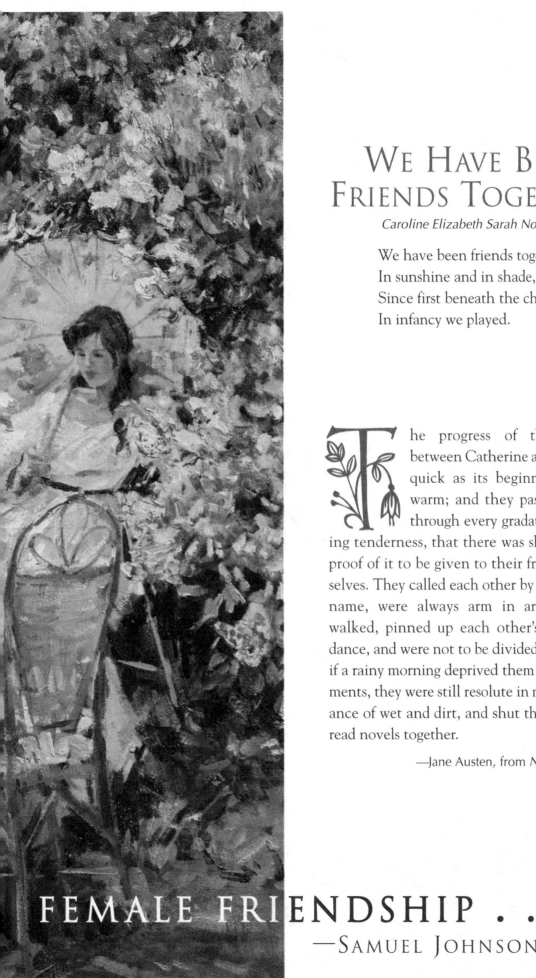

WE HAVE BEEN FRIENDS TOGETHER

Caroline Elizabeth Sarah Norton

We have been friends together,
In sunshine and in shade,
Since first beneath the chestnut trees
In infancy we played.

The progress of the friendship between Catherine and Isabella was quick as its beginning had been warm; and they passed so rapidly through every gradation of increasing tenderness, that there was shortly no fresh proof of it to be given to their friends or themselves. They called each other by their Christian name, were always arm in arm when they walked, pinned up each other's train for the dance, and were not to be divided in the set; and if a rainy morning deprived them of other enjoyments, they were still resolute in meeting in defiance of wet and dirt, and shut themselves up to read novels together.

—Jane Austen, from *Northanger Abbey*

FEMALE FRIENDSHIP . . .
—SAMUEL JOHNSON

Vision by Sweetwater

John Crowe Ransom

It was like a dream of ladies sweeping by
The willows, clouds, deep meadowgrass, and the river.

Robin's sisters and my Aunt's lily daughter
Laughed and talked and tinkled light as wrens.

*Friendship between women
can take different forms.
It can run like a river, quietly and
sustainingly through life; it can be an
intermittent, sometime thing; or it can
explode like a meteor, altering the
atmosphere so that nothing ever feels
or looks the same again.*

—MOLLY HASKELL

Cedar trees line the trail beside the shore of Maidstone Lake in
Maidstone State Park in Vermont. Photograph by William H. Johnson.

A friend hears
the song in my heart
and sings it to me
when my memory fails.
—*Pioneer Girls Leaders' Handbook*

A Friend

Gladys Rappe

A bright sunset may flare and die
Unnoticed by the human eye.
Flowers may grow and bloom and fade,
A gay unheralded parade.
A man may have his work and food
And never think to call it good.
But when a friend, unknown or true,
Extends a helping hand to you,
It strikes a chord complete and strong
That in your heart becomes a song.

The sweetest music is
not in the oratorio,
but in the human voice
when it speaks from its
instant life tones of
tenderness, truth, or courage.
—*Ralph Waldo Emerson*

A harp and a grand piano provide the opportunity for friends to share music together. Photograph by Jessie Walker.

Someone To Remember

Mark Kimball Moulton

At First Sight

I am sure almost everyone is familiar with the expression "Love at first sight," but what about "Friends at first sight"? In this fast-paced, high-tech world, is it still possible for total strangers to share a smile and instantly discover a kindred friend?

I believe it is because it happened to me.

In 1991, I was living an enviably comfortable existence in a small village in Connecticut. During the growing season, I raised multitudes of herbs and flowers for my antique and herb shop. The wintertime found me cross-country skiing or relaxing in front of the woodstove with a pile of seed catalogs and dreaming of brightly colored zinnias and giant pumpkins ripening in the sun.

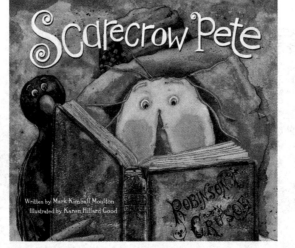

I shared this wonderful life with two lovable dogs, a couple of hardworking cats, several friendly goats who felt it their duty to provide comic relief, and a spattering of laying hens, turkeys, fantailed pigeons, and guinea hens, all suitably housed in and around my 1851 farmhouse overlooking the Farmington River.

My dearest friends lived nearby with my heart's delight, my godchildren; and within walking distance of home was one of the best ice cream shops around with a pick-up window expressly reserved for dogs!

All in all, I was a pretty happy fellow.

But my life was about to be turned upside down, in a good way, by a simple, friendly smile.

In the spring of that year, my partner and I decided to expand our store by including hand-crafted items that would complement our primitive look. We researched trade shows and found one in Pennsylvania that specialized in just these types of wares. We arrived at the show wide-eyed and excited, and we leisurely strolled the aisles inspecting the various offerings and placing orders with discretion. As we turned one particular corner, I felt inexplicably drawn into a booth filled with the most charming whimsical card and calendar art I had ever seen.

But it was not the art that held my attention so much as it was the artist, Karen Hillard Good.

Our eyes locked, and we shared a smile that was as warm and familiar as the summer sun. A moment later we were deeply involved in a conversation that has not ended to this very day.

I had found a kindred spirit.

Since Karen was living in the Midwest at the time, our friendship was initially nurtured by a few shy phone calls using business as a pretense.

These conversations quickly sprouted into daily, often hour-long talk fests on topics that ranged from current events to spirituality to the price of tea in China. Our favorite conversations revolved around books we had recently read, movies we had recently seen, music we simply could not live without, as well as our "everyday heroes." Soon these daily phone conversations were complemented by not-nearly-often enough cross-country visits.

It was during one of Karen's earlier visits that we wrote our first story together, *Conor and His Magic Yellow Pencil, #2*. We were sitting on the riverbank in front of my house having tea and enjoying a silly mood, when we began creating a story about a little boy who finds a magic pencil with which he is able to draw the most wonderful pictures. The story seemed to take on a life of its own as we bantered back and forth that glorious summer day; and we roared with delight at our cleverness and basked in the shared warmth of our friendship.

Eventually Karen took a position with a card company that was seeking to enter the children's book market. The owner asked Karen if she would write a story revolving around a Christmas card she had painted years before with a snowman on the front. I will never forget the night Karen called and asked me to write the story. She prefaced the conversation by saying, "Mark this

day on your calendar. Your life is about to change."

And she was right. In 1999, our first book was published entitled *A Snowman Named Just Bob*, a story written in rhyme about the enduring rewards of friendship. Other books followed in rapid succession. Currently I have fourteen books in publication; and this fall Karen and I will have two more titles, including *A Snowgirl Named Just Sue*, the sequel to our first book.

I still live in the same house that overlooks the river. A flock of chickens still cluck in the backyard, and my fantailed pigeons still coo in the front. But the village has changed. Last August, Karen and her husband relocated here and are currently renovating a handsome brick colonial that sits directly in front of that wonderful ice cream shop with the doggie window. In December, another dream was realized when we opened The Olde Riverton Herbary and Bookshoppe together just down the road.

I cannot imagine what my life would have been like had I not stumbled into that booth. I have serious doubts I would be an author today. I am sure I would not have enjoyed as much laughter and feel as loved as I do. Karen has a saying she is fond of: "Everyone should have five kindred companions—one to keep you humble, one to encourage, and three for socializing." For me, those five kindred companions are all wrapped up in one beautiful gift named Karen.

A
Snowgirl
named Just
Sue

Written by
Mark Kimball Moulton

Illustrated by Karen Hillard Good

READERS' REFLECTIONS

Readers are invited to submit original poetry for possible publication in future issues of
IDEALS. *Please send typed copies only; manuscripts will not be returned. Writers receive
payment for each published submission. Send material to Readers' Reflections, Ideals
Publications, 535 Metroplex Drive, Suite 250, Nashville, Tennessee 37211.*

There Is a Place
Taska Azbell-Pavlas
Lombard, Illinois

There is a place in the shadows of my mind
Where, on occasion, I travel just to find
The sweetest memories of two friends
Sharing conversation and coffee as the day begins.
The subject of talk I can't seem to recall;
The weather or season doesn't matter at all.
It's the time that we spent there sharing our thoughts,
Wondering how many life lessons we've yet to be taught.
This place brings me comfort, a smile that's free.
No matter the distance between you and me,
You'll always be close in spirit and mind,
Somewhere in the shadows where I dwell sometimes.

The Happiest Miser
Douglas Raymond Rose
Grand Prairie, Texas

The happiest miser is the man
Who treasures every friend he can.
May our good friends forever see
More of heaven smiling through me.
May our friendship embrace like a hug
And lovingly give their heart a tug.
Lord, make of me a faithful friend
Upon whose loyalty another can depend.
The happiest miser is the man
Who treasures every friend he can.

Light

Jackie Cavalla
Maspeth, New York

I am light.
    I bring warmth and happiness.
I seek out all places on the earth,
    Even to the depths of the sea.
I am the spark of happiness on the face of a child
    And the glow of remembrance in the eyes of the old.
I shine in the hearts of all men;
    And, though I be hidden from sight,
    The ember still burns,
    Waiting to be rekindled in the look of a friend.

Small Gift

Fanny Washington
Little Rock, Arkansas

A small gift arrived today;
Many would consider it poor,
But your small letter gave me more
Than any surprise in a box:
It brought your dear, kind voice
And memories of evenings we talked
Hours past when students should sleep.
This new letter I now will keep
And hold dear to my heart,
For tonight we'll share words
Though we are miles apart.

My Treasures

Royce Cookson
Hendersonville, North Carolina

I have a thousand pictures
That are near and dear to me;
And when I'm feeling lonesome,
I enjoy their company.

These are my valued treasures,
And I view them one by one.
Then I realize just how wealthy
In this world I have become.

The diamonds are my children
And my wife of many years.
My relatives are all pure gold
Through laughter and through tears.

The silver are my loyal friends
Who are scattered near and far.
They give me joy and gladness.
God protect them where they are.

August Interval

Esther York Burkholder

August is that interval just before fall when summer lingers languidly and minds are still in a vacation mood.

For some of us it is a time of travel, for others a time for catching up on reading or enjoying the old backyard and porch. But nobody is much in a mood for working.

I take my writing to a bench in the shade of our backyard trees, our three cats following at my heels. Bambi, the venerable Siamese, settles himself comfortably on the bench beside me, his blue eyes closing slowly in contentment. Little golden Patrick rolls happily in a flower bed and bats at a passing butterfly, while graceful Delilah bolts her black satin length up a tree and blends with the shadows of the thick branches. They are such good company and so glad to have me share for awhile the outdoor world which is theirs by inheritance.

> **The cat could very well be man's best friend but would never stoop to admitting it.**
>
> —*Doug Larson*

Together we quietly enjoy the afternoon—the light and shadows, the flowers and ferns nodding in the ghost of a welcome breeze, a bird singing nearby. It is all so relaxed and peaceful. We need such intervals in our busy lives.

Maybe that is why August gets so hot. To make us just be lazy for awhile.

Lilies and purple coneflowers surround this retreat in a private garden in Missouri. Photograph by Gay Bumgarner.

My Tiger
O. L. Abbott

He rubs his head against my legs,
He arches up his back,
He does quick rolls upon the floor
Or takes a different tack
By jumping on my lap to purr,
His tail against my chin;
He uses all his bag of tricks
Each time I let him in.
I love these demonstrations,
But do I think them true?
Nobody really owns a cat;
The fact is, he owns you.

Hiding
Emily Brueske

Little Puss and I
Like to hide in the grass
And wonder
About all the things that pass,
Like wind that sings
In the evergreen tree
And puffy white clouds
Floating by in the sky;
Or a ladybug that climbs
A stem
But just can't flit
Like a butterfly.
Then Little Puss reaches
To pat my cheek,
As though she's
Really trying to speak
In her kitten way
To say, "Mew.
It's a wonderful world,
And I love you."

*A young kitten waits not too patiently for her mistress
to play in this painting entitled* In the Garden *by
Henry John Yeend King (1855-1924). Image from
Fine Art Photographic Library Ltd., London/
Courtesy of Anthony Mitchell, Nottingham.*

Dog Wanted

Margaret Mackprang Mackay

I don't want a dog that is wee and effeminate,
Fluffy and peevish and coyly discriminate;
Yapping his wants in querulous tone,
Preferring a cake to a good honest bone.
I don't want a beast that is simply enormous,
Making me feel as obscure as a dormouse
Whenever he hurtles with jubilant paws
On my shoulders and rips with his powerful claws
My sturdiest frocks; the kind of a mammal
That fits in a parlor as well as a camel,
That makes the floor shake underfoot when he treads,
And bumps into tables and bounds over beds.
The sort of pet that I have in my mind
Is a dog of the portable, washable kind;
Not huge and unwieldy, not frilly and silly,
Not sleek and not fuzzy, not fawning, not chilly—
A merry, straightforward, affectionate creature
Who likes me as playmate, respects me as teacher,
And thumps with his tail when he sees me come near
As gladly as if I'd been gone for a year;
Whose eyes, when I praise him, grow warm with elation;
Whose tail droops in shame at my disapprobation;
No pedigreed plaything to win me a cup—
Just a portable, washable, lovable pup!

These I Have Loved

Elizabeth-Ellen Long

These I have loved since I was little:
Wood to build with or to whittle,
Wind in the grass and falling rain,
First leaves along a country lane,
Yellow flowers, cloudy weather,
River-bottom smell, old leather,
Fields newly plowed, young corn in rows,
Back-country roads and cawing crows,
Stone walls with stiles going over,
Daisies, Queen Anne's lace, and clover,
Night tunes of crickets, frog songs too,
Starched cotton cloth, the color blue,
Bells that ring from a white church steeple,
Friendly dogs and friendly people.

A young boy shares a special bond with his "lovable pup."
Photograph by Nancy Matthews.

THE UNLIKELY COMPANION

An interesting passenger rode along with me the other day when I drove to town four miles from home.

Getting in my twenty-year-old automobile, I noticed what I thought was a crumpled leaf on the windshield wiper. Surely it would blow away once I was on the road.

When I started to back the car out of the carport, that crumpled leaf began to take shape and form. The head went high. It was a praying mantis. I expected it would make a quick departure. Instead, he gave me chuckles all the way to town.

For whenever I stepped on the gas pedal and we drove along, this small passenger would bow its head down to its spiny forelegs. But when I eased up on the pedal or had to stop, he raised his head, highly and proudly. The trip included three intersections at which I had to stop and a mile-long stretch down a steep hill. As I drove down the hill, the mantis really hugged those wipers on the windshield. Surprisingly, we were still together at the bottom of the hill.

When I reached the parking area in town, I stopped the car where I could watch the mantis from the window of an office. He made three moves: first to the opposite side of the windshield, then to the top of the car, and finally to the rear, as if he were trying to determine whether the vehicle of his wild ride was still intact. A few minutes later, he departed.

With a smile, I said a silent goodby to this quiet passenger who had entertained me so unexpectedly during our brief journey. And I thought about all the unlikely companions with which life presents us, those who remain with us for longer journeys and those who, like the mantis, touch our lives kindly, but only for a short time.

I realize the praying mantis lowered his head at the car's higher speeds to make him more secure against the buffeting winds. But I really like to think he was in prayer, surely for himself and maybe for that old fellow behind the wheel.

The author of four books, Lansing Christman has contributed to Ideals *for more than thirty years. Mr. Christman has also been published in several American, international, and braille anthologies. He lives in rural South Carolina.*

Ryan's Round Barn is a landmark in Johnson-Sauk Trail State Park, Illinois. Photograph by Terry Donnelly/Donnelly Austin Photography.

Gingham Girls

Edna Staples

The zinnias are gathered on my lawn;
The gingham girls in pinafores so neat
Are whispering low in voices soft and sweet
And reaching heavenward toward the sun;
They'll turn and follow it till day is done.
And if they could in summer free their feet,
I think they'd follow with a dancing beat
And sway and polka with a fancy run.
Their pinafores would flutter in the breeze,
The pretty pinks, the reds, maroons, and blues.
The tangerine, the lilacs, and the rose—
Their blooms would open; and they'd look so pleased
And nod at me to say, "How do you do?"
And I'd smile at the gingham girls' bright clothes.

Last night was cool, the chilliest of the season, and when I went out this morning to look at the flowers I found the bumblebees in the zinnias. That is a good index of the season.

To a bumblebee, a zinnia is more than a flower. It is a bed with a coverlet, protection from the dew and the chill. As I went from one big zinnia flower to another, I ruffled back the petals and found six bumblebees in the first ten flowers, all of them too sluggish and sleepy to resent my intrusion. They had crawled in last evening and let the petals curl back over them, snug as could be. —*Hal Borland*

*The face of the warm, bright world
is the face of a flower.*

—*Algernon Charles Swinburne*

Summer World

Inez Franck

Summer hangs a woodland rainbow,
A clovered kiss of earth and sky.
Fountains dance, the meadows glimmer;
Each rosebud charms a butterfly.

Summer is a heart of moonlight,
A patch of white petunia frills,
Mockingbirds in leafy cadence,
A country wood with whippoorwills.

Summer is a careless moment,
A shaded bend, a sandy beach,
Filling baskets for a picnic
And finding lakes far out of reach.

Picnic

Earle J. Grant

We hike the road for a picnic
This sun-dappled summer day,
Under the lace of willow trees
That trims the winding roadway.

We find a cool spot by the brook
And spread good things to eat
Across a checkered tablecloth—
What a wonderous noontime treat.

We pick blackberries for dessert
And search for rare wildflowers;
We're entertained by sweet birdsong
That floats from nearby bowers.

The sun is sinking in the west;
We head home filled with pleasure,
With memories of this summer day
Stored in our hearts to treasure.

*In this painting entitled RUDOLPH'S MILL
by Bob Pettes, boating, fishing, wading, and
showing off a new car make a sunny day a pleasure.*

A Day Up River
Edith S. Butler

Breathe in this quietness of earth and sky,
The river shining in the summer sun
As wavelets lap the shore and willows sigh;
Such hours, such lovely hours are halcyon.
The sky is very blue this August day;
The lazy white clouds hardly move at all.
I watch two bright green dragonflies at play;
I hear, far off, a crow's discordant call.
The riverbank is edged with pickerelweed,
Blue vervain, and the pearly arrowhead.
A day like this can fill the heart's deep need
For something more than meat and daily bread.
A hidden cricket chirps, a wood thrush sings;
God gives His peace in simple, common things.

The Friendly Brook
Ruby Lee Mitchell

This lazy little brook I saw
Was such a friendly one.
It strolled along all glittery
From playing in the sun.
It had a pleasant chuckle too,
Soft laughter barely heard.
It went its careless, smiling way
As free as any bird.
It toyed with leaves and
    small brown rocks;

It splashed green ferns and reeds.
It gave a drink to bird and beast,
Decked watercress with beads.
I wondered where it wandered to,
Rippling by with joy inside it.
So to find where it was going,
I just strolled along beside it.

Lazy Days
Mrs. Garnet Alley Hampton

The lazy, languid August days
Foretell the misty autumn haze
Which soon the summer sky will glaze.
The locusts call both day and night;
The ants are storing all in sight

As birds prepare for southward flight.
I cannot bring myself to stir
Because on these days I prefer
To drift along and dream awhile
And bask in summer's final smile.

A small brook tumbles over rocks in the South Fork of Elk River in Siskiyou National Forest, Oregon. Photograph by Christopher Talbot Frank.

Fireflies
Punctuate the darkness
With periods of light.
A meteor's dash
Erases its meaning
From the sky's blackboard.
The sum of man's knowledge
Is not equal
To the quiet equation of the stars.
    —Robert Lee Brothers

River Grove

Robert Freeman Bound

We walked along the river grove
One scented August night
And saw the moon's bright scimitar
Etch scenes of pure delight.
We watched the calm and noble elms
Adjust their dusky robes,
Touched with living sequins
Of fireflies' dancing globes.
The poplar trees seemed as candles,
The stars their winking flames,
And the breeze kept us enraptured
With thoughts of far-off names.

Summer's Eve

Neil C. Fitzgerald

The sun moves westward out of sight;
Its warmth remains to greet the night
When sounds of crickets fill the air
And fireflies venture from each lair
To fascinate in unseen flight
Those who watch their twinkling light.
And from the south a gentle breeze
Ruffles the leaves of maple trees
That try to shade the moon's rich glow
As it reflects the porch below,
And folks are reluctant to leave
Enchantments of a summer's eve.

*A willow tree stands gracefully over an array of petunias,
cosmos, verbena, sunflowers, thorn apples, zinnias, and heliotrope.
Photograph by Larry LeFever/Grant Heilman Photography.*

Lamps of Love

June Masters Bacher

Each friend is like a lamp of love
That makes a tiny glow
To shine in every darkened place
My feet may chance to go.

I treat each lamp with tenderness
And trim the wicks with care,
For I would lose my way, I fear,
Unless their light was there.

I polish each with kindly thoughts
And fill it to the brim
With oil of faith that tells my friends
How much I cherish them.

I marvel at their brilliance as
A king with treasures might,
For should I lose one lamp of love
My path would be less bright.

*The Cape Saint George Lighthouse stands tall
and serene at sunset on Saint George Island, Florida.
Photograph by Daniel E. Dempster.*

53

Still all I prize,
Laughter and thought and friends, I have.
—Rupert Brooke

Friendship

Corinne Roosevelt Robinson

Though Love be deeper, Friendship is more wide;
    Like some high plateau stretching limitless,
    It may not feel the ultimate caress
Of sun-kissed peaks, remote and glorified,
But here the light, with gentler winds allied,
    The broad horizon sweeps, till loneliness,
    The cruel tyrant of the soul's distress,
In such sweet company may not abide.
Friendship has vision, though dear Love be blind,
    And swift and full communion in the fair
    Free flight of high and sudden ecstasy,
The broad excursions where, mind knit to mind,
And heart renewed, can all things dare,
    Lit by the fire of perfect sympathy.

Tender and warm the joys of life—
Good friends, the faithful, and the true.
—John Hay

Flowing grasses and cosmos adorn the foreground of this lavender farm hillside in the village of Burton on Vashon Island, Washington. Photograph by Terry Donnelly/Donnelly Austin Photography.

THROUGH MY WINDOW

Pamela Kennedy

LET THE GAMES BEGIN!

Y ou can't use that word!"

"Sure I can. It's a perfectly good word. W-a-z-n-a. I *wazna* able to be at your costume party because my troubadour outfit *wazna* back from the cleaners!"

"Argh!"

"Okay, how about this one? Z-a-w-a-n. As in, 'Is this *zawan* you wanted'?"

"Concede. You lose. You have five leftover letters. There is no hope for you!"

The laughter escalated into squeals as my sons pelted their sister with Scrabble tiles. All in their twenties, they were gathered around the kitchen table engaged in one of their relentless holiday game fests. They are three very different individuals, living three very different lives; but at home, around a board or card game, they bond in laughter and friendly competition as they did when they were younger. We have always been a family that enjoyed playing games. When the children were little, we played Candyland and Cootie at home and countless rhyming and word games in the car where we located colors, out-of-state license plates and called, "I spy . . ." for miles. The games were fun, but there was more going on than just moving plastic pieces on a board or picking out cows as we passed grassy fields. Playing games together encouraged us to give and take, to win and lose gracefully, and to respect one another as individuals.

As the ages of our children increased, so did the complexity of our family games. We began playing Monopoly, Life, and Scrabble, which challenged us to strategize and to think critically. The kids also learned how to get their Dad's goat by scooping up the real estate he had his eye on; and with me, they might claim a double-letter

---

How glad I was that we were not too busy to be silly now and then.

---

score or put down tiles on a word I was planning to use. We had equality around the game board as we all learned to laugh at ourselves, to accept our mistakes, and to enjoy another's victory.

Special occasions have always been a favorite time for games at our house too. Usually, the one celebrating a birthday gets to choose the dinner menu; but I plan the entertainment. Ever since the kids were little, I have enjoyed creating silly games for us all to play at these parties. Although lately college and career responsibilities have kept us apart on many birthdays, a couple of years ago our daughter, Anne, came home for her birthday while on a drama tour, bringing her whole university drama troup with her. All six students and the director stayed at our house for a week. They put on performances and held theater camps during the day and slept on every available surface at night. When I asked if they would like to join in

a family party for Anne's nineteenth birthday, they were all enthusiastic. They even filmed a special video for her, and I went to work figuring out what games we would play.

The night of the party, we gathered around a table decorated with inexpensive plastic toys, colorful streamers, and confetti. Anne donned the obligatory "Birthday Princess" crown, and we dined on her favorite casserole.

Afterward, it was time for our games. The first one was "pilot practice," and everyone flew a small plastic plane off the second floor balcony. It was fun to see who could land their plane closest to the target on the living room floor below. In the next game, teams competed to arrange Anne's school photos in chronological order. After that, we held a "grand prix"; and everyone raced matchbox cars down the middle of the dining room table and tried to keep the cars from dropping off the table's edge. The kids had a great time and so did my husband and I. After the party, while I swept up confetti and took down streamers, one of the girls came into the kitchen to help.

"I couldn't believe you and your husband got right in there with us. That was so cool," she said as she lined up the toy cars on the counter.

"Don't you and your family do silly things together?" I asked.

"Not really. Everyone is so busy. And my parents are pretty serious."

We finished cleaning up, and she joined the others who were watching the birthday video. I sat in the kitchen sipping a cup of coffee. I thought of all the stories these kids would tell about Anne's crazy parents. And then I thought of something else. How glad I was that we were not too busy to be silly now and then. So much of the time we need to be organized and mature. We have to stick to business in work and school. But we also need to remember that it is good to laugh and play together, to create happy shared memories, and not to take ourselves too seriously. Just then, a pink plastic airplane whizzed by my nose. I looked around to see my husband standing in the doorway, a victorious grin on his face. Let the games begin!

Original artwork by Doris Ettlinger.

True Wealth

Fred Toothaker

The world may take away from me
My money or my gold,
The riches that I might have had,
Or treasures I may hold.
My substance may be squandered and
New wealth not be accrued;
I may have missed the chance from which
Prosperity ascends,
But I'll be happy anyhow
Can I but keep some friends.

. . . listening to Jeremy and James, I am transported back to that mint-colored house in that suburban neighborhood. I find myself plunked down in an immense family room with (if memory serves me) a mural of a cityscape painted on its longest wall. If I look to one corner, I see Monopoly gear—the pretty paper money, the little metal hat and dog and shoe, the houses piled up on Broadway and Park Place, a handwritten sign Do Not Disturb. . . .

In front of the couch, in the center of the room, in the midst of my memory stands a wobbly, speckled collapsible table—site of magic shows and Hangman, Crazy Eights and trivia, vast piles of pennies that needed sorting. I can remember sitting there as one of three, being treated as an equal. —Beth Kephart

A game of checkers or marbles and many other indoor pastimes are part of this family room's appeal. Photograph by Jessie Walker.

BITS & PIECES

$\mathcal{W}$herever we are, it is our friends that make our world.

—*Henry Drummond*

$\mathcal{W}$e should talk over the lessons of the day or lose them in Musick, Chess, or the merriments of our family companions. The heart thus lightened, our pillows would be soft, and health and long life would attend the happy scene.

—*Thomas Jefferson*

$\mathcal{L}$ife is a game that must be played:
This truth at least, good friends, we know;
So live and laugh, nor be dismayed.

—*Edwin Arlington Robinson*

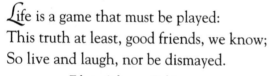

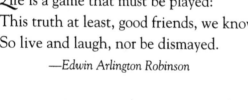

$\mathcal{N}$ow's the time for mirth and play.

—*Christopher Smart*

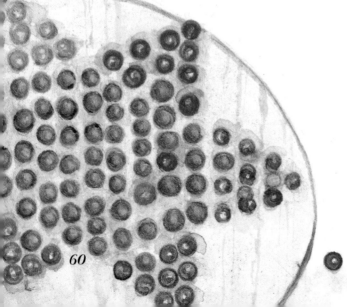

*L*ife is like a game of chess, changing with every move.
—*Chinese Proverb*

*T*he most I can do for my friend
is simply be his friend.
—*Henry David Thoreau*

*T*he kind of fellow I want to know
Is a fellow who's shooting square,
Who plays his game with a steady hand
And always will play it fair.
—*H. Howard Biggar*

*F*rom quiet homes and first beginning,
Out to the undiscovered ends,
There's nothing worth the wear of winning,
But laughter and the love of friends.
—*Hilaire Belloc*

61

FROM AMERICA'S ATTIC

D. Fran Morley

A POPULAR AMERICAN BOARD GAME

Americans have always loved to dream, and perhaps that is why games that allow players an opportunity to become rich, if only while playing the game, have always been popular.

The first commercially produced board game in the United States, The Mansion of Happiness, came out in 1843; it gave players the chance to win eternal happiness through performing good deeds. In 1861, lithographer Milton Bradley designed a game called The Checkered Game of Life; players competed to reach a happy, wealthy old age instead of financial ruin. While still a teenager, George Parker invented and marketed a game called Banking that allowed players to borrow money from a bank and gain pretend wealth through speculation. George loved to create and play games, and it was not long before he formed Parker Brothers with his brother Charles. Years later, during the height of the Depression in 1935, Parker Brothers introduced MONOPOLY®, and its immediate success no doubt reflected those same American dreams of wealth.

Of course, not everyone in America thought money was the route to happiness. According to some historians, MONOPOLY—a game in which the winner monopolizes real estate and industry and bankrupts opponents—is based on Elizabeth J. Magie's 1904 game called The Landlord's Game, a game developed to expose the economic injustices of private land ownership and speculation. Like later versions of MONOPOLY, all players started the game with the same amount of money; and the board featured squares with properties, two utilities,

---

Initially, Parker Brothers rejected the game, saying it took it too long to play.

---

and four railroads, as well as spaces labeled Jail, Go to Jail, and Luxury Tax. Although both games ended with most players broke and one player in control of everything, Magie hoped that those playing her game would see the economic unfairness of monopolies and land ownership to the average person.

Over the next few decades, Magie's game spread by word-of-mouth from one group of friends to another throughout the mid-Atlantic region, and the game's popularity increased as it continued to evolve. High school and college students loved the game and made their own boards, play money, and game tokens. In different communities, players added more railroads, street names, and houses and motels to the board to increase the property values. Eventually, a group of players in the Atlantic City, New Jersey, area began using street names familiar to them, including Boardwalk and Park

Place, names that still appear on modern playing boards.

Yet it was Charles B. Darrow who created the first commercially viable version of MONOPOLY in 1934. Like many others during the Depression, he was unemployed and searching for a way to support his family. At first, he created handmade versions of the game that he played at home with his family and sold a few to friends and other game enthusiasts. But demand for the game was high; realizing MONOPOLY's potential for financial success, he approached Parker Brothers to mass produce the game.

Initially, Parker Brothers rejected the game, saying it took too long to play and had "fifty-two design errors." But Darrow was persistent; and, with help from a friend, he printed five thousand copies that quickly sold out. Soon, Darrow was unable to keep up with demand.

MONOPOLY's success did not go unnoticed by Parker Brothers; and when Darrow went back to the company the next year, Parker Brothers accepted the game. Within its first year of production, MONOPOLY became the best-selling game in America, beating out other games that are still played today, such as Parcheesi and Cribbage.

While the actual origin of Parker Brothers' MONOPOLY may be a bit murky, there is no denying that Charles B. Darrow was clever enough to patent a popular pastime that Parker Brothers successfully marketed.

The America of the 1930s embraced MONOPOLY, perhaps because the game allowed people to escape the difficult conditions of the time, if

Photograph courtesy of Hasbro, Inc. 2005 © Hasbro Inc. Used with permission.

only in their minds. As economic conditions have improved, MONOPOLY continues to be popular; today the standard game is licensed in nearly fifty countries and is printed in twenty-six languages.

The standard MONOPOLY game looks much the same as it did in the 1930s—the property values are the same as they were in 1935; and the taxes have gone up only once, in 1936. That is a good thing too, since players still start the game with only $1,500, which was just about the average yearly American wage in the mid-1930s.

Even though the economy has improved dramatically since people first gathered around the table to play MONOPOLY, players still enjoy escaping into a fantasy world where everyone can become wealthy and own homes and hotels, railroads and utilities. Yes, to many, MONOPOLY still represents the American dream.

D. Fran Morley is a freelance writer and former editor of IDEALS. She and her husband live in Alabama.

IT'S NEVER FAR

Adam N. Reiter

It's never far to an old friend's house,
And the way is smooth and fine;
The path bears many a telltale mark
Of footprints, his and mine.
Each hill and vale and winding curve
Its youthful fancies lend,
And miles are short when I go forth
To the house of an old, old friend.

The day is always bright and fair
When I, on a friend, do call,
Who has been a friend in time and stress
And "stood by" through it all.

Though skies are drear and clouds hang low,
And the outlook's drab and gray;
There's a radiant glow at an old friend's house
That drives the gloom away.

Time never drags at an old friend's house,
And the hours are filled with joy.
He pictures me, I picture him
As a carefree, laughing boy.
Old faces beam with wrinkled smiles,
And the long years brightly blend
In a wealth of treasured memories—
At the house of an old, old friend.

The Sandpiper
Celia Thaxter

Across the narrow beach we flit,
　　One little sandpiper and I,
And fast I gather, bit by bit,
　　The scattered driftwood bleached and dry.
The wild waves reach their hands for it,
　　The wild wind raves, the tide runs high,
As up and down the beach we flit,
　　One little sandpiper and I.

Above our heads the sullen clouds
　　Scud black and swift across the sky;
Like silent ghosts in misty shrouds
　　Stand out the white lighthouses high.
Almost as far as eye can reach
　　I see the close-reefed vessels fly,
As fast we flit along the beach,
　　One little sandpiper and I.

Sandpipers wait for the next wave at East Beach on St. Simons Island, Georgia. Photograph by William H. Johnson.

I watch him as he skims along,
    Uttering his sweet and mournful cry.
He starts not at my fitful song,
    Or flash of fluttering drapery.
He has no thought of any wrong;
    He scans me with a fearless eye:
Staunch friends are we, well tried and strong,
    The little sandpiper and I.

Comrade, where wilt thou be tonight
    When the loosed storm breaks furiously?
My driftwood fire will burn so bright!
    To what warm shelter canst thou fly?
I do not fear for thee, though wroth
    The tempest rushes through the sky:
For are we not God's children both,
    Thou, little sandpiper, and I?

Trout Fishing

Edith Shaw Butler

Pursuing the wary speckled trout,
We followed the brooklet in and out
Of its many winding, crooked turns,
Through shadowed places and waist-high ferns.
Beneath an arching summer sky,
We dangled bait to tempt his eye.
A swift dart and tug at the line—
And he was gone, leaving no sign
Of being there seconds before;
Then we had to turn home once more.
Yet these we shall have for many days:
The scent of crushed mint leaves and the way
Tiny blue forget-me-nots look
Clustered along a pasture brook.

Fishing with a Friend

Robert F. Burgess

A fisherman's day is filled with all the fierce moods of outdoors, the laughing waters, and the idle chuckle of an outboard on a summer day. The day starts with cloudless skies and a lulling ride across the lake, up the river, and into the sloughs. Fishing is the sport where nobody cares what time it is or how late it gets. Nobody notices sunburned arms because troubles and worries are swept away by the deep waters hurrying to the sea.

The day is best shared with a friend. The fish are hitting up the rivers; they are bedding in the lakes; the surge and call of the surf is strong in the air. Then comes the sudden tug of the line, the quickening of the heart, the whispered whir of the reel, the limber arch of the rod, and the great throbbing that follows a first long run. The give and take, the straight lunge, the tackle-busting dive, the surprise leaps, the first sight of flaring gills and silver scales are relived with each shared recollection.

Fishing is the sport of the long white beaches, the wild rumble of breakers, the cake-frosting combers, the stiff-legged sandpipers. It is the sport of anticipation, the immense and salty smell of the sea, and the hope for luck.

A friend makes the luck good, no matter the howl of the wind or the smell of thunder. The going, the trying, the hoping, and later the story of the big one that got away—a friend shares them all.

Poles and bright rain boots are kept handy for the next fishing trip. Photograph by Jessie Walker.

Overleaf: The foliage is beginning to wear autumn's colors at Chapel Falls in Pictured Rocks National Lakeshore, Michigan. Photograph by Carr Clifton.

HOMETOWN AMERICA

Melissa Lester

ELBA, ALABAMA

"Mama, when will we be there?" my four-year-old son asked impatiently.

"Soon, Darling," I replied. As we traveled through little towns and across acres of farmland, Carson counted cows along the way while his younger brother, Christian, slept.

Carson looked inquisitively at a roadside produce stand. "They have boiled peanuts for sale," I explained.

"What are boiled peanuts?" he asked. I could only shake my head.

For so long, I had looked forward to introducing my children to Elba, Alabama, a charming southern town that was as much a character in the story of my childhood as the people who lived there. Settlers began developing the town around 1840. The name was chosen in 1851 at a town meeting where all present were allowed to drop a name into a large top hat. The name drawn was suggested by a man who was reading a biography of Napoleon Bonaparte, who had been exiled to the island of Elba. In the more than 150 years since, the population has grown to about four thousand.

Finally, my boys would experience Elba. The ladies class at the church where my father had served as minister was beginning a study of my recent book, and the ladies had invited me to return to share a meal and teach the first class.

As we drove into town, I told my sons stories about my hometown's rich history. Elba is a place of fierce community spirit, the kind borne out of perseverance through difficult times. Elba sits where the Beaverdam Creek, Whitewater Creek, and the Pea River merge. The town has experienced four floods in its history, and townspeople view the watermarks inside the county courthouse as a testament to the town's strength. "Elba is the only city I know of with rules on the books against riding your boat around the square," residents would declare with a smile. As a schoolgirl, I had always been fascinated by tales of the 1929 flood, on record as Elba's worst flood event.

As we reached the church building, happy

As we drove into town, I told my sons stories about my hometown's rich history.

---

memories filled my mind: eating boiled peanuts, the favorite way for locals to enjoy one of the area's prime agricultural products; playing during recess on the levee that surrounded the city; riding bikes through the neighborhood; joining the whole town on Friday nights to cheer the fighting Tigers to victory on the high-school football field.

Once inside the church, my sons and I were met with hugs from my lifelong friends. Just as I remembered, Carolyn Brunson was still the epitome of a gracious southern lady. The longtime widow of a respected judge, Mrs. Brunson was the matriarch of her family. As a young girl, I was certain she must be the best cook and most hospitable person in the county. We caught up on events of the last few years as she arranged heaping platters of food for that night's potluck. I told Mrs. Brunson how I had always aspired to practice hospitality as she did. And we both laughed as I told her how I had attempted to make her classic chicken potpie as a newlywed, not knowing that the "sweet milk" her recipe called for was just regular milk and not sweetened condensed milk.

I also spoke with Mrs. Stephens, a lovely, petite lady who used to drive me home after I babysat for her children. Whenever I call a babysitter, I always think of her and hope that I can be a Mrs. Stephens to the teenage girls we welcome into our home.

And what a privilege it was for me to present my favorite teacher, Mrs. Killingsworth, a signed copy of my first book; for it was she who nurtured my love of writing during ninth and tenth grade English.

These women and others filled the audience for my Elba homecoming. What a special moment it was to finally stand before this group of genteel southern women—former neighbors, teachers, and classmates. As I began my lecture, I was so thankful for Elba and the people who are the heart of the town. Looking into the proud faces of so many who, by their examples and encouragement, helped me throughout adolescence, I realized that one of the greatest blessings

The Coffee County Courthouse and the graceful fountain nearby are a source a pride for the local community in Elba. Photograph by Moseley's Photography.

of growing up in a small town is that people see you not just as you are, but as the person you can become.

While I presented my lecture, the boys played outside at the church playground. Their laughter filled the twilight as they caught lightning bugs with a few other children; and it seemed just yesterday that my sister, brother, and I played these same games after church. Finally, the children came inside, smelling of honeysuckle and red clay. Although my boys were exhausted, sweaty, and dirty, they looked so happy, so content. So at home.

As we drove away, I reminisced about my small town home and the blessings of being welcomed again. I thought the boys were fast asleep until Carson's voice broke the silence. "Mama, when can we go back to Elba?"

"Soon, Darling," I replied. "Very soon."

Walking to School
D. A. Hoover

Walking to school down goldenrod byways,
Chorus of blackbirds in frost-painted trees,
Swinging a dinner pail, hearing the crickets,
Feeling the crispness of September's breeze,
Hearing bell music beyond the horizon,
Down in the valley, the one-room red school—
Warm in my heart are these sweet, childhood memories
When life was pure joy with a few simple rules.

*Friendship happened in
neighborhoods and classrooms
and lasted for seconds and years.
It turned trees into castles
and marbles into coins,
the streamers on a tricycle
into wings of plastic glory.*
—Beth Kephart

Little Red School
Robert P. Tristram Coffin

The little house where boys and girls
Sat with heavy heart,
The red house with the single room
Was where we got our start.

Very close to corn and truth,
To cows and all creation,
America sat with naked feet
And learned to be a nation.

*According to legend, Mary Sawyer, whose lamb was the inspiration
for the well-known nursery rhyme, attended school accompanied by her
pet at this red schoolhouse. The school was recently moved to
Sudbury, Massachusetts. Photograph by William H. Johnson.*

Friendship Tapestry

Mildred C. Higgins

Beautiful and rich is old friendship;
Like a tapestry threaded with gold,
It shines through the years in splendor
With patterns striking and bold:
Laughter and words softly spoken,
And handclasps warm and true,
Nearness in comforting silence
At times when sorrow comes through.

Pleasures, smiles, and successes
Are woven in threads of song
To brighten the hearts of comrades
As they travel the roads along.
May our friendship ever smolder
With life's warm, tender glow;
And may we meet again like this
And peace and laughter know.

Class Reunion

Mary E. Linton

I shall go back again along the trail
My feet once followed when the heart was young.
There is something the years cannot assail
That beckons backward when old songs are sung.
I shall walk quietly through streets grown strange
And hear familiar echoes call my name.
Time is perceived alone through growth and change;
The years leave little that remains the same.

Another generation's feet now walk
The same old path and find it ever new.
Someday they too will gather here to talk
Of life grown rich because this path was true.
Following onward, still the heart will know
Always the road leads back, and I must go.

Big leaf maples in the Washington Park
Arboretum in Seattle, Washington, provide
a breathtaking foretaste of the full spectrum of autumn colors.
Photograph by Terry Donnelly/Donnelly Austin Photography.

79

There is magic in the autumn sunrise:
The frost in its infancy, like powdered sugar sprinkled on a hot cake,
The whiteness momentary;
The quiet of the dawn, breathless with each awakening;
The heavy dew tracing designs on the leas with sparkling pearls;
The cobwebs in the grass, soon to be floating in the air.
Yes, there is magic and a revelation in an autumn sunrise.

—Helen Nencka

September Morning
Betty Hunter

Now dance the shadows
Between the rows of corn;
Rustling leaves whisper
Across the faded lawn;
Yesterday butterflies
Flew in careless flight,
And fireflies filled the meadow
With scintillating light.
First frost comes tonight,
And stars wink winter warning;
Yet warm is the kiss
Of Autumn's golden morning.

The softness of an autumn sunrise ascends the Blackwater River in the Canaan Valley of West Virginia. Photograph by Carr Clifton.

ON AUTUMN'S DOORSTEP

Edith M. Helstern

Tomatoes are red-ripe and plump;
Green peppers shine in the sun;
Apples are red on bending branches;
And the harvest has begun.
Wild grapes swing in bunches
Like jewels on a vine,
And feathery heads of goldenrod
Stand out along a line.
Mornings are cool and moist;
The change of autumn is in the air;
High noon is a time of mellow warmth;
On autumn's doorstep, September is here.

Autumn has caught us in our summer wear.

—Philip Larkin

GOLDENROD'S WEALTH

Annette Swearingen

Fall has arrived; and goldenrod,
Many hearts sing praises
For your radiant, lacy nod
On these special autumn days.
Some say you cause a constant sneeze,
But they still love you dearly;
You wave with every passing breeze,
Renewing friendships yearly.

You humbly choose the fields as home,
But proudly bear your banner;
Above the drying grass and loam,
You reign in regal manner.
Surely the name of goldenrod
Was given for a reason:
Your gold proclaims the wealth of God
All through the autumn season.

Goldenrod and asters pair their lovely colors along this field in Bristol, New Hampshire. Photograph by William H. Johnson.

Inset: A goldfinch landing on a perfectly matched frond of goldenrod is one of nature's special sights. Photograph by Gay Bumgarner.

Simple Things

Margaret Hasbargen

Give me the simple things again:
The sumac's slow September red,
The magic of fall's smoke haze spread,
The fragrance sweet of baking bread,
The blend of voices that I know,
The rooster's urgent rousing crow,
A kerosene lamp's drowsy glow,
The wind-stirred whisper of a pine,
Clusters of grapes upon the vine,
The comfort of a couch that's mine,
The valley churchbell's soft refrain,
The measured rhythm of the rain
Against a starchy-curtained pane,
The piercing boil of brine and spice,
The purring current under ice,
A fresh-air freedom without price,
The beauty of a rainbow spun,
The flow of wheat fields in the sun,
The homing herd when day is done,
The sweet perfume of clover hay,
The starlit song that follows day
When sunset softly fades away.

Give me the simple things again.
More than a chapter from the past,
All these are memories to last,
Within my joyful heart held fast.

The brilliant red foliage of a maple contrasts with the soft yellow fall dress of birches near Plum Lake in Northern-Highland American Legion State Forest, Vilas County, Wisconsin. Photograph by Mary Liz Austin/Donnelly Austin Photography.

READERS' FORUM

Snapshots from our IDEALS readers

Left: "Allie's Bobtails"—Snuggled together for an afternoon nap, these five (Yes, there are five!) kittens are natural bobtails. This charming snapshot was sent to us by Tammy Jones of Eastland, Texas.

Below left: SpongeBob adores his young playmate, Anna McDaniel. She is the granddaughter of Dee J. McDaniel and Marj McNeal of Scottsbluff, Nebraska.

Below right: Maurice, who resides with Retha McCarty in Gladstone, Missouri, has deep, deep thoughts about the recent snowfall.

Top left: Fluffy is a three-year-old yellow Labrador retriever. Brenda Knable of Bagley, Minnesota, writes us that her family found him abandoned at a horse auction when he was just a puppy. He soon became her son Paul's best friend.

Top right: Shane, a tenth-month-old English setter, cuddles with his best friend, Possum. These contented friends are the pets of Diane Johns of South Berwick, Maine.

Right: Sharon Walker of Tifton, Georgia, shares this snapshot of Muffin amid the rabbits.

THANK YOU for sharing your favorite pet snapshots with *Ideals.* Each one we received had a wonderful story. Remember to send us your favorite Chistmas snapshot for the Christmas issue.

We invite readers to share precious children's photographs with the *Ideals* family. Please include a self-addressed, stamped envelope if you would like them returned; or keep your originals for safe-keeping and send duplicates along with your name, address, and telephone number to:

Readers' Forum
Ideals Publications
535 Metroplex Drive, Suite 250
Nashville, Tennessee 37211

Dear Reader,

When we think of *friendship*, we usually reflect on our childhoods. And the memories of those years can be precious. As an only child, I had to depend on neighborhood children for playmates and there were many, fortunately, on Pennsylvania Avenue where I grew up. We played almost daily after school before organized activities took claim in later years. Each of us felt as comfortable in one another's yards and inside one another's homes as we did in our own.

Certain memories have a special place in my heart. My first co-conspirator, Austin, and I plucked green tomatoes from a grouchy neighbor's garden; Celia and Letitia, both accomplished musicians as adults, led our impromptu choruses. We were fascinated with the shining ripples of Samar's knee-length hair as it swayed with her steps. On hot afternoons, Colonel Harris mesmerized us with tales of exotic places as we crowded his porch. And all of us were chaperoned by Freckles, Judy's brown and white cocker spaniel, and by my collie, Puddles. We belonged to several different churches and made certain that each of our friends were included when the youth socials were hayrides or cookouts.

These early friendships have proven to be unaffected by distance and the passage of years. They are solid and reliable in the whirlwind of adult life. When my daughter was born, Judy gave me a pink crocheted sweater with matching bonnet and booties which her mother had made and Judy had to set aside when she had three boys. When Samar returned home for her parents' sixtieth anniversary, I was enchanted that she still had that beautiful hair.

No matter how varied our life paths, today we share the memories of those moments that established us as kindred spirits. May the golden days of autumn bring more friends into your life.

Marjorie L. Lloyd

ideals

Publisher, Patricia A. Pingry
Editor, Marjorie Lloyd
Senior Designer, Marisa Calvin
Copy Editor, Marie Brown
Permissions Editor, Patsy Jay
Contributing Writers, Lansing Christman, Joan Donaldson, Melissa Lester, D. Fran Morley, Mark Kimball Moulton

ACKNOWLEDGMENTS

BACHER, JUNE MASTERS. "Lamps of Love" and "Moments to Cherish." Used by permission of George W. Bacher. BORLAND, HAL. An excerpt from *This Hill, This Valley*, Copyright © 1957 by Hal Borland. Used by permission of Frances Collin, Literary Agent. BRUESKE, EMILY. "Hiding" from *Our Little Friend*. By Emily Bruske, 1973. Used by permission of Pacific Press. BUTLER, EDITH SHAW. "A Day Up River" and "Trout Fishing." Used by permission of Nancy B. Truesdell. FRANCK, INEZ. "Summer World." Used by permission of Caroline F. Stevens. HELSTERN, EDITH. "On Autumn's Doorstep." Used by permission of Virginia J. Cooper. KEPHART, BETH. Excerpts from *Into the Tangle of Friendship: A Memoir of the Things that Matter*. Copyright © 2000 by Beth Kephart. Reprinted by permission of Houghton Mifflin Company. KLEMME, MINNIE. "The Tree." Used by permission of Herbert L. Klemme. LINTON, MARY E. "Class Reunion." Used by permission of Richard W. Kobelt. MACKAY, MARGARET MACKPRANG. "Dog Wanted" from *The Saturday Evening Post*. RANSOM, JOHN CROWE. An Excerpt from "Vision by Sweetwater" from *Two Gentlemen in Bonds* by John Crowe Ransom. Copyright © 1927 by Alfred A. Knopf Inc., a division of Random House. RORKE, MARGARET L. "Friends." Used by permission of Margaret Ann Rorke. We sincerely thank those authors, or their heirs, some of whom we were unable to locate, who submitted original poems or articles to *Ideals* for publication. Every possible effort has been made to acknowledge ownership of material used.

Pages 26 and 27: Two friends share a quiet moment in a garden in a painting by Viktor Yefimenko entitled LILAC BLOSSOM. *Image from Fine Art Photographic Library, Ltd., London/Holland & Bourne Gallery Reigate/Art Gallery Gérard, Wassenaar.*

Inside back cover: Letters are shared by friends in this painting entitled NEWS FROM ABROAD *by Henry John Yeend King (1855-1924). Image from Fine Art Photographic Library Ltd., London/Courtesy of Haynes Fine Art, Broadway.*

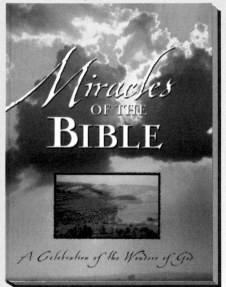

A Celebration of the Wonders of God

A fascinating look at the many accounts of the Bible's Miracles.

Miracles of the Bible is a breathtakingly beautiful book illustrating dozens of awe-inspiring miracles chronicled throughout the Bible. Passages from the Old and New Testaments are accompanied by page after page of contemporary photographs of the places where the miracles are thought to have taken place. Specially created maps of the Holy Land, along with stunning photographs of the sites as they are today, make this a fascinating book for the entire family.

Travel throughout the land of Moses and Aaron ...

Through the Sinai Desert, past the Great Pyramids in Egypt, and along the Nile River. Then on through the wilderness, and across the River Jordan and into the promised land.

And in the footsteps of Jesus and His Disciples ...

Follow His path along the Sea of Galilee, through Cana, Nazareth, and the Old City of Jerusalem to the joyous site of His resurrection. This inspiring, faith-filled journey is one your whole family will enjoy.

Do you wish the Bible was a bigger part of your daily life?

If you would like to make the Bible truly come alive, this lovely booklet—developed especially for preferred customers like you—is yours FREE for the asking. Receive your free gift copy of *Bless the Day* simply by accepting a 21-Day Preview of *Miracles of the Bible*.

This beautiful booklet of daily devotionals is yours to enjoy— ABSOLUTELY FREE!

Simply return the reply card today to preview *Miracles of the Bible* for 21 days FREE. . . . and receive a FREE *Bless the Day* booklet.

FREE EXAMINATION CERTIFICATE

YES! I'd like to examine *Miracles of the Bible* for 21 days FREE. If after 21 days I am not delighted with it, I may return it and owe nothing. If I decide to keep it, I will be billed $24.95, plus shipping and processing. In either case, the FREE *Bless the Day* booklet is mine to keep.

Total copies ordered _____

Please print your name and address:

_____
NAME

_____
ADDRESS   APT#

_____
CITY   STATE   ZIP

Allow 4 weeks for delivery. Orders subject to credit approval.
Send no money now. We will bill you later.
www.IdealsBooks.com   15/202341261

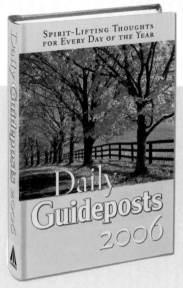

SPIRIT-LIFTING THOUGHTS
FOR EVERY DAY OF THE YEAR

Daily Guideposts 2006

GREAT IS THY FAITHFULNESS

No matter what may happen in the world around us, whether our own life's journey seems like a brisk walk on a smooth road or a difficult climb up a steep mountain path, God is our faithful Companion all along the way. And so our theme for *Daily Guideposts, 2006*—our thirtieth edition—is "*Great Is Thy Faithfulness.*"

Every day of 2006, you'll find an invitation to renewed faith, a peaceful heart, and confident living in *Daily Guideposts, 2006*. Every day, you'll share Scripture, prayer and an insightful story of God's grace at work in our world with all the members of our *Daily Guideposts* family. And every day, you'll grow in gratitude to the One who is always with us to strengthen, comfort and inspire. Truly, great is His faithfulness!

Here's the best part:

In just five minutes a day, you will find the spiritual richness in your own life throughout the year. Join us as a part of a remarkable family of readers and writers brought together by a common faith and united by heartfelt prayer. You will be moved by the following series:

* **Daily Guideposts Classics**
* **The Smallest of Seeds**
* **Turning Points**
* **Grace Notes**
* **Hope on the Road**
* **The Hardest Good-bye**
* **Comfort in Our Grief**
* **A Hidden Glory**

Plus, learn more about the authors and readers, like you, in the "Fellowship Corner" and "Reader's Room." Keep a monthly journal and more.

Return the Free Examination Certificate today to preview *Daily Guideposts, 2006* for 30 days FREE . . . and receive a FREE *Scripture Bookmark*.

FREE EXAMINATION CERTIFICATE

YES! I'd like to examine *Daily Guideposts 2006*, at no risk or obligation. If I decide to keep the book, I will be billed later at the low Guideposts price of only $14.95, plus shipping and processing. If not completely satisfied, I may return the book within 30 days and owe nothing. The FREE *Scripture Bookmark* is mine to keep no matter what I decide.

Total copies ordered: _____

❏ Regular Print ❏ Large Print
  (Hard cover)   (Soft cover)

Please print your name and address:

_____
NAME

_____
ADDRESS   APT#

_____
CITY   STATE   ZIP

Allow 4 weeks for delivery. Orders subject to credit approval.
Send no money now. We will bill you later.
www.guideposts.org

Printed in USA
16/202341259

Your Free
SCRIPTURE
BOOKMARK
just for ordering.

I am with thee, and will keep thee in all places whither thou goest....
—Genesis 28:15 (KJV)

No need to send money now!